To

Father Benedict Horvath
with respect & admiration

Yours

ICONOGRAPHY

ON THE MOUNT OF OLIVES OVERLOOKING JERUSALEM

During his trip around the world, in 1961 the author settled for some fifteen days on the Mount of Olives as a pilgrim. Here he became aware of St. Birgitta as a pilgrim, mystic and a great religious leader. This awareness led to this second volume.

ICONOGRAPHY

ST. BIRGITTA OF SWEDEN

BY ANTHONY BUTKOVICH

ROSÁN, INC.

ECUMENICAL FOUNDATION OF AMERICA

1969

Table of Contents

Preface

In the army of Christ, the saints are His heroes. Although all the saints excel in their virtues, some saints can be called saints of the saints. The authors favored saints are St. Bernard of Clairvaux, St. Birgitta of Sweden, and St. Ignatius Loyola. Their personal lives exemplified heroic self-denial, they were committed to the cause of Christ and His Church, and they were involved with their world in a constructive way. As mystics they meditated on the Passion of Our Lord and the Sorrows of Our Lady, as leaders they were aware of Christian Knighthood as an outcome of their continued striving towards human perfection, and as warriors of Christ they were intrepid in combating heresies in defense of Mother Church. St. Birgitta was a devotee of St. Bernard and St. Ignatius an admirer of St. Birgitta. Yet, all three were linked by a spiritual bond through the centuries in upholding the Christian tradition. One thing surely they had in common: an absolute obedience to the Vicar of Christ.

During his fifteen months tour around the world, the author made his pilgrimage to the Holy Land. Here on the Mount of Olives at the very place where Our Lord lamented over Jerusalem, his awareness of St. Birgitta came to light. A fascination with a beautiful Swedish princess — the richest woman of all Scandinavia, a mother of eight children and prematurely a widow, who decided to give her life to Christ — led to the Trilogy on St. Birgitta of Sweden.

The first volume, Anima Eroica (Heroic Soul), presented a comprehensive biography of her seventy years of life dedicated to the Church and her fellow man. The second volume, Iconography, as a pictorial biography expands and complements the previous one. The third volume, The Revelations, will be an abridged edition of some thousand pages of her visions, which greatly influenced the Christian world. Although these three volumes represent a unity, each separate volume stands as a complete work.

Each volume required a special visit to Europe in search of precious material in numerous churches, museums and libraries. It is indeed a great satisfaction to publish some reproductions of art for the first time. To take them out of dark corners of churches and museums and thereby redeeming the works of almost forgotten masters.

These volumes are published by the Ecumenical Foundation of America, which is founded on the ideals of St. Birgitta in striving for Christian unity. St. Birgitta traditionally was considered a patron saint of Christian nobility. Today she could be regarded as a patroness of social leadership. Therefore, let us hope that the life and work of St. Birgitta may serve as a source of inspiration to the spiritual and social leadership in the world of today, a time which so much resembles St. Birgitta's own century.

Popes and Emperors, Kings and Cardinals, Saints and discoverers and artists admired St. Birgitta and followed her footsteps, as dramatized in this Iconography. Her personal life was heroic, her prophetic Revelations were sent all over Europe, and her stand in favor of Christian unity under One Shepherd makes her a "Saint for all seasons." St. Birgitta is as contemporary today as she was in her own century.

On this occasion I would like to express my gratitude to the Swedish scholars Andreas Lindblom, Prof. Henrik Cornell, Sven Stolpe and Dr. Hans Cnattingius for their assistance; and to all churches, museums, and libraries involved in this project where patience proved to be a virtue.

My special gratitude to *Don José and Charlotte Mary Rosán,* whose great love and devotion to St. Birgitta made this volume possible, and my filial devotion to the *Right Reverend Monsignor P. Peter Canisius van Lierde,* Vicar General of His Holiness, whose blessings from the heart of the Vatican, inspired my work.

ANTHONY BUTKOVICH

Los Angeles, December 25, 1968

Chapter I

THE MYSTIC OF THE NORTH

Guido Fulignot, XX C.   Private Collection, Los Angeles

MYSTICAL FRIENDSHIP THROUGH THE CROSS

(St. Brigid of Ireland and St. Birgitta of Sweden)

The Mystic of the North

Before the decisive battle at the Milvian Bridge the Emperor Constantine the Great had a vision of a Cross over the sky. In this sign of the Cross he achieved victory over the West. As a great gesture he issued the Edict of Milan in 313 proclaiming the Christians free. The echo of the Crucifixion finally embraced the Roman Empire and the temples of Jupiter and Venus started to tremble. The pagan civilization was about to be replaced by Christianity.

Almost a thousand years later in the North, King Erik of Sweden raised his banner with a red Cross on a golden ground proclaiming the victory over the pagans. The Viking temples of Thor and Frey crumbled under the onslaught of the new believers with the Bible in one hand and the sword in another. The decisive battle raged around Old Uppsala, where the legendary temple of Valhalla perished in flames with all its gods and heroes.

On the ground of the old pagan temples and anointed with the blood of the first martyrs, the Christian Church was born. But just as the civilization of Western Europe was a product of the hard labor of the Benedictine Order, whose monasteries served as the first parishes, schools, agricultural stations, and social gatherings, similarly in Scandinavia the missionaries started to convert the pagans and the mendicant orders established the first monasteries as religious, cultural, and social centers. Among them the most important were the Cistercian Monastery at Alvastra, the Domenican Monastery at Skänninge, the Franciscan Monastery at Stockholm, and later the Birgittine Monastery of Vadstena. But the symbolic victory of Christianity was the majestic cathedral in the old capital of Sweden, Uppsala, overlooking the fields and the hills of Uppland. Only a few miles outside of Uppsala was a castle of Finsta where a girl by the name of Birgitta was to be born.

The conversion and pacification of Scandinavia was accomplished by the national kings and the local princes. In the popular mind, King St. Olaf and King St. Erik replaced the pagan gods Thor and Frey.

3

Missionaries and the monastic orders introduced the rudiments of Christian education. The royal family of Folkunghi introduced feudalism, the orders of chivalry, and Western culture into Sweden. And now in the fulness of time Sweden was ready for the first national, canonized saint: St. Birgitta.

Her parents, Sir Birger and Lady Ingeborg Persson, were related to the royal family of Folkunghi. Sir Birger was a princeps of the most important province of Uppland. The first Christian law was written and codified by Sir Birger. The Cathedral of Uppsala, the resting place of most Swedish kings and princes, was built by the Persson family. For generations, the Perssons had been pilgriming to Jerusalem, Rome and Compostella. There is a legend about a shipwreck from which Lady Ingeborg was saved miraculously "in order to give birth to the child whose wondrous voice will be heard all over the world." The Perssons were returning from their favored Saint Brigid of Kildare pilgrimage in Ireland. In such a religious atmosphere a gentle but indomitable Birgitta was born in the year 1303 of Our Lord. Like a Northern Star she was to shine over Europe.

The religious character and the strictness of her family life were shaping little Birgitta. The Swedish climate of cold, long and dark winters and the lush, green, and vigorous springs somehow influence the person mystically. Birgitta had her first great religious experience when she was eleven years old. One night, after listening to a Domenican preacher speak on the Passion of Christ in the Cathedral of Uppsala, she had a vision of Our Lord Crucified so dramatically vivid that this experience became a turning point in her life. This vision was to be surpassed only at Golgotha when she was an old woman.

Education started at home and Birgitta enjoyed the cultural atmosphere of her parents, people well read and traveled. Her father was a statesman and the most prominent man in the kingdom. Private tutors advised by Bishop Brynolf of Algot, the first Swedish poet in the Latin language, imparted the rudiments of education to Birgitta. Bishop Brynolf was related to the royal family and studied at the Sorbonne and later was proclaimed a saint. Birgitta's spiritual director was Master Matthias, a dean of the Linköping Cathedral, graduate of the Sorbonne and a man of letters. Under the influence of Birgitta he translated the Pentateuch into Swedish. Birgitta acquired the basic Latin language from Bishop Niels Hermansson, a graduate of Sorbonne and a poet. Finally Prior Peter Olafsson of the Cistercian monastery of Alvastra gave to Birgitta religious and historical knowledge. At a later date, Bishop Alphonse Pecha de Vadaterra of Jaen exerted a great theological influence over Birgitta. Her education was built into her apostolate throughout her life.

It was customary during the Middle Ages for the princely families to arrange the marriages of their children. After her mother, Lady Ingeborg died, Birgitta spent the rest of her childhood at the court of her aunt Catherine in Ostrogothland. Birgitta's father decided to marry his daughter to Prince Ulf of Nericia. Her dream was to become a nun, but the will of a strong father prevailed and obedience was a virtue in the Persson family. The young couple lived for two years in voluntary abstinence, then had a large family of eight children. Among them, the best known were, St. Catherine of Sweden, romantic Sir Karl who died in Naples, Martha, a lifelong friend of the great Queen Margareth of Three Kingdoms, and the chivalric Sir Birger who followed his mother as far as Jerusalem. The strictness of Birgitta as a mother became proverbial in Sweden. In many ways this marriage reminds one of St. Elisabeth who married the landgrave of Thuringia at the age of fifteen. Both St. Elisabeth and St. Birgitta were Tertiaries of St. Francis.

The young King Magnus Eriksson, whom Birgitta's father held at Baptism, ascended the throne. The old guard of advisers was replaced by the new courtiers, among them Prince Ulf of Nericia. They found a wife for the King in Countess Blanche de Namur of Flanders. On the insistence of the royal couple, Birgitta moved to the Court where she advised the King in matters of social justice. After all, Birgitta was a daughter of the first Christian lawman of Sweden. When the Crown Prince was baptized, Birgitta held him at the altar as his godmother. But the courtiers around the young Queen Blanche exercised a frivolous influence on the royal pair. Although King Magnus as a cousin of Birgitta consented in giving her the land and the Castle of Vadstena for the Birgittine monastery, the life of the royal couple became so ludicrous that Birgitta and Prince Ulf left for pilgrimages. Both were Tertiaries of St. Francis.

Leaving the royal court at Stockholm, Birgitta and her husband found themselves free. Their daily life at their castle of Ulfasa was semi-monastic. The time was spent in prayers and meditations on the Passion of Christ, social work in taking care of the private hospital, the hospice for the aged and widows, and the orphanage for abandoned children. They took care of monasteries and churches and even recruited young women for convents. Every Thursday Birgitta fed some twelve poor men and washed their feet in memory of the Last Supper.

Being a true daughter of her religious parents, pilgrimages were food for her mystical soul. For the Medieval Christian Jerusalem was a crown, Rome and Compostella were the jewels. The first pilgrimage was to the shrine of St. Olaf at Nidaros over the Norwegian Alps. Could Birgitta at this point have dreamt that one day she would be venerated together with St. Olaf? The next pilgrimage took Birgitta over half of Europe following the "Roads of the Kings" to St. James of Compostella. Here Birgitta became aware of the semi-monastic and semi-military Order of St. James protecting the tomb. On the way back home Prince Ulf fell ill in Arras, France. Prince Ulf survived his illness and true to his promise entered the Cistercian monastery at Alvastra. Shortly afterwards, however, he died and Birgitta found herself free from terrestrial ties. For two years she stayed at the monastery at the tomb of her beloved husband in ardent prayers, meditations and mortifications asking the Lord to show her the road. Here Christ appeared to her accepting her as His bride. With a new sense of mission Birgitta returned to the royal court which had greatly changed through deterioration of morals. Her warning against the gluttony and drunkeness were scoffed at as "moralizing by a mad woman." She warned that it was a time for repentance and that the Black Pest was at the door of Sweden. And then again in the grand gesture of a biblical figure Birgitta decided "that the further she journeyed for the love of God from her own country, the nearer she would come to heaven." Birgitta left for the heart of Christendom: Eternal Rome. Sweden escorted her in tears, for to most good people Birgitta was already a saint.

And so Birgitta left Kalmar, a rich Hansa city with its scenic castle. The road led over Stralsund, Cologne, Altmünster, Milano and Genova to Rome. She arrived in Rome in the autumn of 1349 on the eve of the Holy Year proclaimed by Clement VI, very much at her insistence. Birgitta was accompanied by a retinue of confessors, secretaries, knights and ladies. Her visions in Arras and Alvastra to come to Rome were fulfilled and her apostolate was about to begin.

6

R. Werner, XX C.   Stockholm

THE FIRST APPARITION OF OUR LADY

"Piety seemed to possess Birgitta in its very perfection even from the cradle. At the early age of seven, God began to favor her with His communications, which became more frequent as she grew in age." (J. E. Darras, A General History of the Catholic Church)

Medieval Art, XV C.   Stockholm

THE FIRST APPARITION OF CHRIST

Ever since Birgitta had her first vision of Our Lord speaking to her, Christ's Passion became the dominant theme of her Revelations which in turn greatly influenced the Western religious mind.

Biagio Puccini, XVIII C.   Domus Birgittae, Rome

AMOR MEUS CRUCIFIXUS EST

To combat the dechristianization of a Sweden that worshiped the golden calf, the lust of the flesh and the pride of the devil, Birgitta needed a living Christ in her heart. Christ was her love.

Medieval Art, XV C.   Stockholm

PILGRIMAGE TO ST. OLAF

*The first pilgrimage Birgitta undertook with her husband over the snowy
mountains to the venerable shrine of St. Olaf, patron saint of Norway. Today,
the bearded St. Olaf symbolized with the Axe, and St. Birgitta with her Book,
are patrons of Scandinavia.*

Titian, XVI C.   Prado, Madrid

PILGRIMAGE TO ST. JAMES OF COMPOSTELLA

On the second great pilgrimage Birgitta traveled with her husband over half of Europe to far away Spain to the shrine of the Apostle St. James of Compostella. Today St. James, the patron saint of Spain, and St. Birgitta, the patron saint of Sweden, both are patron saints of pilgrims.

Biagio Puccini, XVIII C.   Domus Birgittae, Rome

IN THE FOOTSTEPS OF OUR LORD

Every Thursday Princess Birgitta received in her castle twelve poor men, fed them abundantly, mended their clothes, and washed their feet in memory of Christ at the Last Supper. Indeed Birgitta followed the sign of the Cross.

Chapter II

ANGEL OF ROME

Woodcut, XV C.   Nuremberg

PATRONESS OF THE PILGRIMS

Angel of Rome

Birgitta arrived at Monte Mario overlooking the Vatican and the whole panorama of the Eternal City. A year before, an earthquake had added a few more ruins to Rome and even St. Peter's Basilica was damaged. The earthquake and the Black Pest which came from the East, brought the already low morals even lower. Birgitta lamented, "Oh Rome, Rome, be converted and turn to the Lord thy God." The City was divided between two feuding families, pro-papal Princes Orsini and pro-emperor Princes Colonna. And the vision of Christ in Alvastra asking Birgitta to leave for Rome came true.

During her first days Birgitta stayed at the same tavern of Ursi where exactly fifty years before the great Dante had lodged during his Holy Year pilgrimage. Birgitta and Dante used biblical language in dramatizing their world. Both condemned the "great sinners of Avignon," as did Petrarca later. Cardinal Hugo de Beaufort, a nephew of Pope Clement VI, on hearing of the distinguished Princess Birgitta of Sweden, graciously offered his palace at St. Lawrence of Damasso. Today this palace, reconstructed by Bramante, serves as the Chancery of the Church in Rome. In an adjacent Church there is an altar fresco of St. Birgitta.

The first thing Birgitta did was to visit St. Peter's Basilica, where over the tomb of the Apostle she ardently prayed for the Romans. Here she had a vision of St. Peter telling her "she will live long enough to see the vicegerent of the Church coming back to Rome." Indeed Pope Urban V returned to Rome in 1367. Then she visited the rest of the Seven Pilgrims Churches of Rome. Her favorite was St. Paul's Basilica Outside the Walls, where the miraculous Cross of Cavallini spoke to her. Every Roman knows of St. Birgitta's Cross. Before this Cross, St. Ignatius Loyola took his last vow.

Besides visiting her favorite churches, Birgitta served in the hospital during the epidemics of the Black Pest. She especially took care of the pilgrims from Scandinavia who arrived for the Holy Year. Birgitta performed miracles in healing the sick. By healing Prince Gentile

Orsini she befriended the family of Orsini, whose association became decisive for the rest of her life in Italy. The Orsinis were the most influential family in Rome and gave many Cardinals and a Pope to the Church. Prince Niccolo Orsini served as a good will ambassador for Birgitta in arranging audiences with Pope Urban V at Montefiascone. Through the centuries, St. Birgitta has been a family saint of the Orsinis and in their palaces there has always been a Chapel of St. Birgitta. In the Orsini family there was a "ring of St. Birgitta," given always by the father to the oldest son.

Birgitta was less interested in the ruins of the past, rather she was more interested in the future of the Church. She was not interested in the political struggle between the powerful families and the political tribune Cola di Rienzi. Rienzi proscribed many aristocratic families and established the Republic. Birgitta admired the great Spanish Cardinal-soldier Egidius Alvarez Albornoz, who was sent by Pope Clement VI to pacify the warring local princes either by diplomacy or by force. The great Cardinal Albornoz whose Constitutiones Egidiane served as a model constitution for the Papal States until the XIX century, established the peace throughout Italy. He outplayed the powerful families in Rome through Cola de Rienzi only to remove him when he became too difficult. Cardinal Albornoz had a special regard for the Bishop Alphonse of Jaen, whom he introduced to Birgitta. Bishop Alphonse became confessor to Birgitta and was responsible for editing Revelations. Another Spaniard who became a follower of Birgitta was General Gomez Albornoz, Duke of Spoletto and nephew of the Cardinal.

Because of her saintly life in Rome, Birgitta was truly loved by friends and admired even by her enemies. God always takes care of his true servants and it was a great help to Birgitta when her daughter Catherine arrived from Sweden. They settled in the little palace of the Countess Papazurri. The Roman aristocracy tried to involve Birgitta in partisan politics, but she stayed neutral. Birgitta met the poet laureate Petrarca at an audience with Pope Urban V as arranged by Prince Orsini. She had no interest in pagan-minded Boccaccio and his De-cameron which praised the virtues of the flesh instead of the delights of the spirit. The Decameron was set in the courtyard of the famous S. Maria Novella Church in Florence. Later, a disciple of Lorenzetti set a great fresco of the Annunciation on the wall of this Church. In a very corner of the Nativity scene he placed Birgitta kneeling in adoration. In a way, Boccaccio and Birgitta crossed their paths in the cultural history of Italy.

Settled at Campo di Fiori in the heart of old Rome which belonged to Prince Orsini, Birgitta could plan to make new pilgrimages. Already on her journey to Rome she had visited the tombs of the great St. Ambrose in Milano who had so gallantly stood up against the arrogant Emperor Theodosius at the door of the cathedral. Now Birgitta stood up against the worldly Archbishop Visconti reminding him of the words of Ambrose, "Humilitas." Some clergy, more concerned about life on this earth than about saving the souls of their flock, were proposing freedom to marry. Birgitta adamantly upheld traditional clerical celibacy. In Pavia she visited the tomb of the great St. Augustine, who is with St. Thomas Aquinas a pillar of the Church. St. Augustine sinned as a young man, repented as a mature man, and served the rest of his life to the greater glory of God. In Piacenza Birgitta visited a cathedral with a famous Crucifix, Volto Santo. In Genova, Birgitta stayed at the faubourg Quarto where Columbus was born over a century later. Columbus often climbed the steep hills to the Birgittine monastery.

At the tomb of St. Francis of Assisi, Birgitta could meditate on the great saint and reformer who gave up the leisures of this world in order to harvest the fruits in heaven. Here she became aware of two gentle servants of God, St. Francis and St. Clare, whose friendship truly served the Church for centuries to come. There is a tradition that Birgitta visited the tomb of the great teacher St. Dominic in Bologna. In San Petronio's Basilica there is an altar fresco of Birgitta.

Now the road led down South of the Bel Paese, as Italians would call it, "where the lemons blossom and the cypress bend under the Mediterranean breeze." Birgitta, no longer young, climbed the forbidding mountain of Monte Gargano to visit the shrine of the Archangel Michael and prayed "Holy Michael Archangel defend us in the day of battle, that we will not be lost on the day of judgement." In Bari, Birgitta with her retinue of friends of God visited the cathedral of St. Nicholas, protector of sailors and children. His name brought memories of Christmas stories in snow covered Sweden. In Salerno, Birgitta prayed at the tomb of the Apostle Matthew, a good publican who "when God called him, threw off the heavy burden of the world and instead took upon him the light yoke of Christ." Present at the Passion of Christ he later became the great Evangelist. Pope Gregory VII, who loved freedom so much that he preferred to die in exile, is buried close to the Apostle. Birgitta reached a dreamy Amalfi where Goethe, Longfellow and Browning composed their verses. There too Richard Wagner searched for his final tunes for his last work Parsifal in order to find his own Holy Grail of redemption. The proud Republic of Amalfi founded the Order of St. John of Jerusalem, known today as Malta, and codified the first maritime law. In the cathedral of Amalfi, similar to the ones in Siena and Florence, lies buried the Apostle St. Andrew, whom St. John the Baptist called "Agnus Dei." Above Amalfi there is a ghostly tower of the ruins where passionate Queen Giovanna was imprisoned before being strangled by her enemies. Birgitta and Giovanna were friends, but two different lives led to two different ends.

In the old Roman town of Benevento, Birgitta visited the tomb of St. Bartolomew the Apostle and in Ortona sul Mare visited the tomb of St. Thomas the Apostle. St. Augustine said "Thomas first did not believe, in order that later we can believe." Finally Birgitta reached aristocratic Naples, city of passion and romance which changed eight kingdoms in eight hundred years. Birgitta stayed at the court of the beautiful Queen Giovanna. Here Birgitta made friends with all the leading families, Orsini, Acciaiuoli, Caraffa, Pignatelli, Caracciolo, San Severino and Sabran. Birgitta's saintly life converted many to the right path of God, miraculously healed many sick, and exorcised the devil out of sinners. At the court she attacked the women who through abortions prevented God's creation. Many repentant knights and ladies followed Birgitta's footsteps, and there is a strong tradition that the Knighthood of St. Birgitta was conceived in Castle D'Anjou. The families of Naples who kept the tradition of St. Birgitta alive assembled in 1859 and reconstituted the Knighthood of St. Birgitta.

Birgitta was on her way to the Holy Land to fulfill the dream of every Christian. At Cyprus she met Queen Eleanor and warned the Greeks to return to the One Shepherd before the Turks would end the Eastern Roman Empire. Cyprus, the island of Venus, lived the life of Gomorrah and was crushed at first by the Genovese and later by the Turks as Birgitta had prophesied. The glory of Birgitta's pilgrimage was at Golgotha where as an old woman she could now relieve the Passion of Christ "echoing the hammer strokes over the nails on the Cross." In Bethlehem, Birgitta could hear Our Lady conveying to her in lyric sweetness the story of the Nativity. Birgitta felt that her earthly road was coming to an end and, advised by a voice from heaven, she hurried back to Rome in order to bring the Pope back from Avignon.

Biagio Puccini, XVIII C.   Domus Birgittae, Rome

VISION OF ST. AGNES

In Rome St. Birgitta had a vision of St. Agnes bestowing upon her a golden crown with seven precious stones as a reward for her seven virtues. However, St. Birgitta preferred a crown of thorns in memory of Our Lord.

Paolo Vetri, XX C.   St. Birgitta Church, Naples

A LADY OF CHARITY

Princess Birgitta as a grand dame of the royal court established a private hospital, a hospice for the aged and an orphanage for abandoned children, always taking personal interest in the poor as a true Samaritan. (Pietro Chiminelli, La Mistica del Nord)

Baldassare Peruzzi, XVI C.   St. Maria della Pace, Rome

BIRGITTA SPONSORING A WEALTHY DONOR

"The elderly Knights, tired of the hardships of the world, against suitable gifts, sought the peace and quiet of the monastery. They entered there as worldly brothers, and kept on using their titles as Knights." (K. Löfström, Sweriges Riddarordnar)

Medieval Art, XV C.   Vadstena, Sweden
THE CARDINALS AND BIRGITTA

"Saint Birgitta is the most illustrious pilgrim that lived within the Walls of Rome . . . this woman of royal blood, the energetic counselor of four popes was certainly one of the greatest religious women who ever lived." (E. D. Theseider, History of Rome)

German Renaissance, XV C.   Nuremberg

THE EMPEROR, THE POPE AND BIRGITTA

"Birgitta was of an indomitable, aristocratic spirit, always remaining the noblewoman to whom it was natural to speak the truth to the princes of State and Church." (V. Nilsson, History of Sweden)

Atilio Palombi, XIX C.   Domus Birgittae, Rome

A MIRACLE IN THE HEART OF ROME

St. Catherine of Sweden for whom the Pope Urban VI said "she indeed drank her mother's milk", followed her saintly mother Birgitta in performing miracles such as stopping the raging flood of the Tiber river in Rome.

Chapter III

APOTHEOSIS

C. Galle XVIII C.   Vatican

GOD'S AMBASSADRESS

Apotheosis

In the Middle Ages the dream of every true Christian was to die in Jerusalem in the land sanctified by the Master. Birgitta heard a voice from
heaven commanding her to accomplish her mission in Rome. Under
way she stopped again in Naples, once a city of pleasure, but now of tears
because the Black Pest had decimated the population. At the court of
Queen Giovanna, Birgitta lashed out against the courtesans because
of their painting their faces and fitting their clothes so tightly as to entice
the sensuality of men, and equally reproaching the chevaliers for their
short and immodest attire. The brillant gathering of ladies and knights
was deeply moved by this heroic soul whose whole life was dedicated to
Christ and humanity. Birgitta was already considered a saint in Naples
and three churches carried her portraits. Later several Popes and Cardinals from Naples participated in her canonization. Returning to Rome
Birgitta sent her last message to Pope Gregory XI at Avignon, "for love
of Christ to return." At the same time the young Domenican, Catherine
of Siena wrote her first message to the Pope.

But only in the Middle Ages was it possible to be at home in Stockholm as well as in Rome. The same Church, the same official Latin
language, the same system of Universities. Spiritually, one could speak
of the United States of Europe. Only in such an Europe could Birgitta,
inspired by Christ, send Bishop Hemming of Åbo with a message to the
Kings of England and France to end their fratricidal war. Only in such
an Europe could Birgitta find herself in the heart of Christendom and
demand of the Pope that he leave Avignon and return to Rome.

Birgitta felt that her life was at an end and for the last time visited
the Seven Pilgrims Churches of Rome. The most intrepid pilgrim after
the Apostle Paul, Birgitta lightened the path for another pilgrim, the
ecumenical Pope Paul VI. The Apostle Paul wrote his Epistles, Birgitta
her Revelations and Pope Paul VI has carried the living word of God
through all the continents. All three faced a changing and revolutionary
world, but regardless of difficulties they prevailed.

Birgitta on her deathbed, was preoccupied with one thought dear to her, "what will become of her monastery of Vadstena?" Christ appeared to Birgitta assuring her that "she will be accounted as nun and Abbess of Vadstena." Her last dream was fulfilled. Birgitta called on her daughter Catherine and gave her the last advice, "Patience and silence." The small group of her friends who accompanied her throughout her apostolate of twenty-five years in Italy, assembled around her. She was dressed in her religious habit and placed on the table on which she had written so many divine messages. As she received Holy Communion she departed, "Into Your hands, O Lord, I am committing my spirit." Seventy years of service to God ended on this earth to begin another in heaven. Birgitta was known as "God's ambassadress," "Christ's secretary," "Mystic of the North," and "Fulfiller of the New Testament."

The death of the Angel of Rome struck the Eternal City like lightning. In fourteenth century Rome Birgitta's Revelations were released by her secretary as a sort of bulletin. Birgitta's name enjoyed great authority ever since her prophecy, that Pope Urban V and Emperor Charles IV would meet in Rome, came true. Her humility and motherly goodness toward the poor, the sick and the aged were proverbial. Everyone had recognized her as she walked with a pilgrim staff visiting the churches of Rome. The most powerful families of Rome had competed for her saintly presence and friendship. A mere touch of her hand and a prayer could heal the sick or drive the demon out of the heart of a sinner.

In front of the Domus Birgittae on the present Piazza Farnese there was a tumult of Romans who wanted to pay their last homage to her. The funeral was delayed for several days because masses wanted to see her and even touch her for the last time. Even at this last moment God granted miracles through the touch of Birgitta as recorded by the Clarissian nun of the family Savelli. Temporarily Birgitta was buried in her favorite Church of St. Lawrence in Panisperna where she often visited the Clarissian nuns. There is a story telling how Birgitta humbled herself by begging in front of St. Maria Maggiore in order to help these poor nuns.

The final cortege escorted Birgitta outside the walls of Rome accompanied by the Cardinals and the clergy of Rome, and followed by Sir Birger and her daughter Catherine, Bishop Alphonse, Prior Peter Olafsson, Princes Orsini, Colonna, Savelli, Frangipani, Ottaviani and many more. The cortege reached Ancona then continued by boat to Trieste and through Austria, Moravia, Germany and Poland to Danzig and over the Baltic to Sweden. At the door of the majestic cathedral of

Linköping, Bishop Hermansson, once a tutor of Birgitta's children, delivered the eulogy ending with his own poem, "Rosa rorans bonitatem, Stella stillans claritatem, Birgitta vas gratiae." Exactly a year after her death her remains reached the final destination, her monastery of Vadstena. Sweden received her with tears, as it had let her go with tears, some twenty-five years before. Only now she returned as a heroine of the nation. With her returned her friends, now already old people, who faithfully had served in her apostolate. During her lifetime Birgitta stood before Popes and Kings, Princes and Cardinals as well as poor people, always with the courage of an indomitable biblical figure and it was not difficult to predict that "she will be honored by later generations which in far future will praise her name."

Immediately the process of canonization had been initiated. King Albrecht of Sweden sent a deputation to Rome urging the canonization based on historical datas of Birgitta's life, work and miracles. The same proposal came from Queen Giovanna of Naples, who although she loved the pleasures of this world, yearned for the saintly spirit of Birgitta. Pope Gregory XI, although still in Avignon, authorized the ecclesiastical authorities in Sweden to proceed with the investigation of Birgitta's life. Archbishop Bernardi of Naples, a gentle soul who worshipped Birgitta, instituted a regular canonical procedure for canonization. Catherine, her daughter, and Birgitta's confessors and secretaries, worked feverishly in assembling all the pertinent material for the commission. Except for a Schism which broke out in 1378, Birgitta would have been canonized immediately. The Curia Romana opened the official process with the commission of several cardinals and theologians. Unfortunately, Gregory XI died, and Urban VI, a great devotee of Birgitta, plunged into the turmoil of the Western Schism, which interrupted the canonization. In the meantime many friends of Birgitta died, her daughter Catherine, Prior Peter Olafsson, Bishop Alphonse, Bishop Hermansson and even her son, Sir Birger. In 1391, Pope Boniface IX, a Neapolitan and great admirer of Birgitta, with a Bullum "Ab Origine Mundi" officially proclaimed Birgitta a canonized saint with a feastday on October 8. A "great sinner and anti-Pope John XXIII," also a Neapolitan, who became a great devotee of Birgitta, knowing that her intercession with Our Lord was efficacious, wanted to reconfirm the canonization at the ecumenical Council of Constance in 1415. He expiated his sins in great penitence evoking St. Birgitta and died in Florence. King Erik XIII, who married Phillipa, sister of King Henry V of England, insisted on reconfirmation by Pope Martin V. The Pope confirmed the canonization with the Bullum "Excellentium Principum."

In 1396, at the National Council of Arbog, convened by Queen Margareth of Sweden, Norway and Denmark, St. Birgitta was proclaimed the patron saint of Sweden. Birgitta who used to pray over the tomb of St. Erik, a patron saint of Sweden, joined him as a co-patroness. Her follower St. Catherine of Siena joined St. Francis of Assisi as a co-patroness of Italy. A life conceived in the heart of old Sweden, outside of Uppsala, where the battle between pagans and Christians took place around the legendary Valhalla, was chosen by Providence to become a Northern star to shine all over Europe. In 1889 the astronomer Wolff of Heidelberg named a star after St. Birgitta. But her spiritual light shone much stronger through her legacy left to posterity.

Pope Urban VI proclaimed the Cult of St. Birgitta which spread all over Europe in the XIV century. In England there was a Cult of St. Birgitta until the reign of Elisabeth I and the persecutions. In 1891 Pope Leo XIII acknowledged St. Birgitta's cult. This Cult of St. Birgitta centered on the Rosary of St. Birgitta, The Five Wounds of Christ Devotion, and Fifteen Oh Jesus prayers. In Sweden, although Lutheran since 1559, there is still great love for St. Birgitta, and ecumenical minded Archbishop of Uppsala, Nathan Söderblom, founded Societas Sanctae Birgittae. In 1968 Cardinal Eugene Tisserant visited Uppsala saying, "St. Birgitta is a bridge between Catholic Rome and the Protestant North."

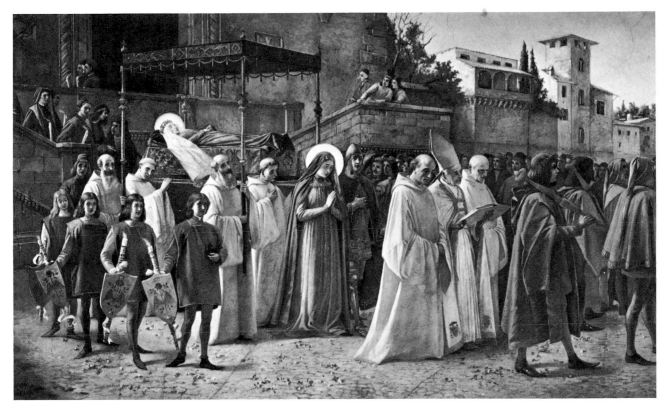

Atilio Palombi, XIX C.   Domus Birgittae, Rome

PILGRIMAGE TO THE HEAVENLY JERUSALEM

Rome of the XIV century was a city of anger and hate, tumults and revolts and cold hearts. Yet when St. Birgitta died, Rome suddenly realized that its very conscience was struck. Never before had Rome shed tears as at the funeral of St. Birgitta, their "Angel of Rome."

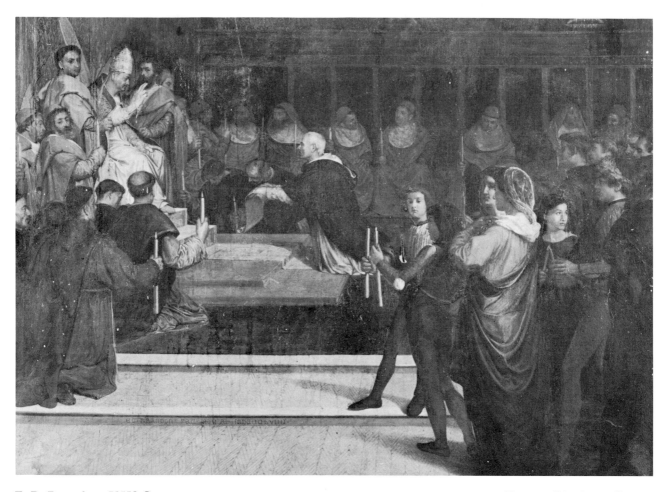

E. D. Brandon, XIX C.   Domus Birgittae, Rome

CANONIZATION OF ST. BIRGITTA

Only eighteen years after her death, Birgitta was canonized by Pope Boni-
face IX with the Bullum "Ab Origine Mundi" in 1391, at the initiative of
Queen Margareth of Sweden, Norway and Denmark.

Luca Giordano, XVII C.   St. Birgitta Church, Naples

APOTHEOSIS OF ST. BIRGITTA

St. Birgitta dominated the XIV century. She advised popes and kings, instituted religious and knightly orders, and wrote a Book of Revelations. After her, churches, monasteries, mountains, rivers and even a star in heaven were named.

Fra Angelico, XV C.   Florence

ST. BIRGITTA AMONG THE SAINTS

"Virginity merits crown, widowhood draws near to God, matrimony does not exclude from heaven." (St. Birgitta)

Chapter IV

THE BOOK OF REVELATIONS

Stefano Maderno, XVI C.   St. Paul's Basilica, Rome

A PROPHETESS

The Book of Revelations

The Revelations of St. Birgitta are a major work of religious literature in the Western world, written by a great religious leader who did not dispute the Gospel but lived by it. Her Revelations are written in biblical style and gravity. Some admirers have wanted to incorporate them as an addition to the New Testament. In the Bullum of Canonization, Pope Boniface IX declared that "the Revelations are inspired by the prophetic spirit." Birgitta was called an instrument of God through whom God spoke to the world.

During her two years retreat in the Cistercian monastery of Alvastra, Birgitta had a vision of Christ accepting her as His bride: "And I say to thee, thou shalt be My bride and it shall be through thee that I will speak to the world." (Extrav. 92) Birgitta, greatly concerned about the state of affairs of Sweden and its morals, declared "the Son of God will visit the Kingdom with the sword and lance and with wrath." Birgitta was announcing the oncoming Black Pest as Christ had told her: "I shall plough the field with my wrath and pull the bushes and trees by their roots. Where a thousand people lived, barely a hundred will be left." (Extrav. 74) Indeed the prophecy came true and half of Sweden was harvested by the plague. Similarly, Birgitta prophesied the end of the royal family of Folkunghi because of their un-Christian life.

In Arras during her pilgrimage to St. James of Compostella, St. Denis appeared to Birgitta indicating her future pilgrimages to Rome and Jerusalem. The same vision was repeated in Alvastra: "Go to Rome . . . and stay in Rome until you see the Pope and the Emperor together, and then you shall proclaim My words to them." (Rev. Extrav. 8) Birgitta had a similar Revelation in St. Peter's Basilica on her arrival in Rome in 1349: "I tell thee that thou shalt live long enough to see with your own eyes My vice-gerent come back to Rome, and thou shalt hear the people cry: Long live the Pope." (Rev. IV, 5) Indeed, Pope Urban V arrived in 1367, and Emperor Charles IV of the Holy Roman Empire established peace and friendship. Pope Urban V stayed in Rome until 1370 when under the influence of the French cardinals he returned to Avignon. He hardly put his foot on French soil when he died, as Birgitta had prophesied. Urban V died in his Benedictine habit asking Birgitta for forgiveness.

The next Pope Gregory XI, again a Frenchman, was a friend of Birgitta. But attachment to this world can make even a Pope vacillate. Birgitta insisted on Gregory's return after a vision which told her, "it is the will of God that he shall humbly bring the Chair of Peter back to Rome." Under the influence of the French cardinals, Pope Gregory XI did not follow her advice. Prince Orsini transmitted another Revelation which read: "If Pope Gregory does not come to Rome at this time, everything that he now possesses in Italy shall be torn assunder and given to his enemies. And then he will not be able to regain it." (Rev. IV, 40) The Papal States with Rome were surrounded by enemies. From her deathbed Birgitta sent her last message to Gregory: "O Rome, Rome, the Pope despises you and does not count my words for anything. Therefore shall he no longer hear the sound of my music." (Rev. VII, 31) Gregory XI finally decided to return in 1378.

The Hundred Years War raged between England and France. Edward III of England ascended the throne in 1327 and disregarded the summons of Phillip VI of France to render feudal homage for the Duchy of Acquitane. Through Phillip IV, Edward III as King of England was directly related to the House of Capetians, whereas Phillip VI was related through the collateral House of Valois. Edward III made his dynastic claims by the force of arms. Birgitta called the war "a fratricidal war."

After the battle of Crecy, which decimated the French aristocracy, Birgitta sent Bishop Hemming of Åbo to intervene between the courts of France and England suggesting intermarriage. After the battle of Agincourt in 1415, King Henry V of England followed Birgitta's Revelation and married Princess Catherine of Valois. (Rev. IV, 105) Except for the appearance of Joan of Arc and the final victory of France, both Kingdoms would have been united under one crown.

The Babylonian Captivity of the Papacy hardly ended when another misfortune befell the Church: the Great Western Schism. It was not a doctrinal dispute in the Church, but the question of the lawful election of Pope Urban VI. At first there were two popes, Urban VI and Clement VII. Then followed John XXIII, and Gregory XII and Benedict XIII. On the insistence of Emperor Sigismund, the Schism which was prophesied by Birgitta in her Book of Revelations, IV, 48, was ended by the election of the Pope Martin V.

During her pilgrimage to the Holy Land, Birgitta stopped at Cyprus. The island reminded one of Sodom and Gomorrah where the goddess Venus ruled. Queen Eleanor, like Blanche and Giovanna pretended to repent. Birgitta thundered like an Old Testament prophetess: "I will destroy this generation and its seed upon whole Cyprus, I will spare none, neither rich nor poor . . . and afterwards I will plant a new vineyard in Cyprus, a people who will keep My commandments and love Me with all their hearts." (Rev. VII, 19) Cyprus was conquered at first by the Genovese and then by the Turks.

The Schism, pertaining to doctrine and jurisdiction, started with the Greek Orthodox Church in the XI century. Such a division of Christendom was unbearable to the ecumenically-minded Birgitta. Her Revelations warn the Greeks to come into the one fold under One Shepherd, otherwise "the Byzantine Empire will perish before long." (Rev. VII, 19) At the Council of Florence Pope Eugenius IV tried to heal the wounds of separation between Rome and Constantinople. Too late. In 1453 the Eastern Roman Empire fell into the hands of the Infidels as Birgitta had prophesied.

In the Holy Land at the grotto where Our Lady was born, Birgitta had a vision of the Immaculate Conception, "Ego concepta fui sine peccato originali," and of Our Lady's Assumption into Heaven. (Rev. VI, 61) The Immaculate Conception was declared a dogma in 1854 by Pius IX and the Assumption by Pius XII in 1950 as St. Birgitta prophesied.

Among the last Revelations Birgitta had were: "Papal State of the Vatican as a sovereign and independent state centered around St. Peter's Basilica, Hospital of the Holy Spirit and Castle of San Angelo surrounded all by the walls." (Rev. VI) In 1929 the Lateran Treaty was signed between the Vatican and the Kingdom of Italy guaranteeing the Vatican's sovereignty. Not the Lateran Palace, but the Vatican became the definite seat of the popes.

To Birgitta the most important Revelation was "Regula Sancti Salvatoris" in Book VII, in which Christ commanded her to found a new and national religious Order of the Most Holy Saviour as a double monastery. Birgitta was inspired by the Order of Fontevrault in France and by the Gilbertines in England to found a double monastery. The Order was approved by Pope Urban V at Montefiascone in 1370 by giving it the Augustinian rules and Birgittine constitution as a subsidiary. Since the Lateran Council in 1215 the Church did not approve the new rules. Jurisdiction was in the hands of the Abbess General and the spiritual guidance of the Father Confessor General. The Birgittine Order was predominantly for nuns, priests and brothers serving as spiritual advisers. Just as the Apostles had cared for Our Lord's Mother Mary. All the monasteries had the name of Mary, as Triumph of Mary, Fountain of Mary, Heaven of Mary, Paradise of Mary, etc. The most important monasteries were, the Mother Monastery of Vadstena, which became a religious and cultural center of Sweden in the late Middle Ages until the Reformation. The monastery "Paradise of Mary and Birgittae" in Florence was built by the nobleman Antonio degli Alberti. In Genoa "The Heavenly Path of Mary and Birgittae" which exercised a great spiritual influence on many, including Columbus. The largest and richest monastery in England was "Immaculate Conception and Birgitta" in Syon near London built by King Henry V. It was a religious and cultural center during the XV century from which the Cult of St. Birgitta spread over England. The Birgittine monk, Blessed Richard Reynolds, preceded Sir Thomas More to the scaffold for the defense of the Faith. Queen Margareth of the Three Kingdoms built the monastery in Maribo, Denmark. In Poland "Marientriumph" was built by the thankful Poles after the victory over the Teutonic Order in 1410 at Tannenberg as Birgitta prophesied. Today there are Birgittine monasteries and convents all over Sweden, Denmark, Finland, Norway, Germany, Poland, France, England, Italy, Holland, Belgium, Spain, Portugal, Mexico, India and the United States of America. A noble lady Marina de Escobar founded the Spanish-speaking branch of the Birgittine Order in the XVII century with the houses in Spain and Mexico. The Swedish convert, Maria Elisabeth Hesselblad, reconstituted the traditional Birgittine Order in the XX century as a modern order with its headquarter in Piazza Farnese, Rome. Today's Abbess General is dynamic Mother Hilaria Laubenberger. Special attention should be paid to the beautiful Convent of St. Birgitta at Vikingsborg in Darien, Connecticut, which is a favorite ecumenical retreat house for New Yorkers.

The Religious Order of the Most Holy Saviour, known popularly as Birgittines, stands for Christian Unity, regeneration of the truly Christian life and charity towards one's fellow man. There is hope for the expansion of this noble order in the Western hemisphere.

Brussels School, XV C.   Frankfurt

WRITING THE REVELATIONS

"Les Révélations sont variées, et certaines d'une poésie admirable, parfois même d'un lyrisme sublime, tel le récit des éblouissantes visions de Jérusalem. Birgitta a laissé des traces durables dans l'histoire de L'Église et de la litérature religieuse." (La Litérature Suedoise, 1957)

Giuseppe Montanari, XVIII C.   In Panisperna, Rome

CHRIST SPEAKING TO BIRGITTA

"And I say to thee thou shalt be my bride and it shall be through thee that I will speak to the world." (Rev. Extr. 92)

Italian Baroque, XVIII C.   Domus Birgittae, Rome

A MESSAGE FROM HEAVEN

"Tu eris Sponsa Mea et canale Meum et audies et videbis spiritualia, et spiritus Meus permanebit tecum usque ad mortem." (Rev. Extr. 47)

Fra Bartolomeo, XVI C.   Accademia, Florence

BIRGITTA BESTOWS THE RULES

*In order to regenerate the spiritual and moral life of Sweden and Europe,
Birgitta founded in 1346 a Religious Order of the Holy Saviour in Vadstena
as a "double monastery for nuns and monks."*

Spanish Baroque, XVIII C.   Domus Birgittae, Rome

THE BIRGITTINES IN SPAIN

The Birgittines were introduced into Spain in the beginning of the seventeenth century by Blessed Marina de Escobar. This branch of the Order of St. Birgitta bears the name Recollection and was approved by the Pope Urban VIII.

Matteo di Giovanni, XV C.   Vatican

GREGORY XI RETURNS TO ROME

"O Pope, return to Rome! Christ wants you!" were the last words of St. Birgitta ending her twenty-five years of apostolate in Rome. Birgitta could only rejoice from Heaven at seeing her successor St. Catherine of Siena bring the Pope back from Avignon.

Chapter V

NATIVITY OF CHRIST

Herman Rode, XV C.   Stockholm

THE BRIDE OF CHRIST

Nativity of Christ

In the Book of Revelations, Birgitta prophesied the Black Pest in Sweden, the return of the Pope from the Babilonian Captivity in Avignon, friendship between the Pope and the Emperor of the Holy Roman Empire, the Great Western Schism in Christendom, the Fall of the Eastern Roman Empire with Constantinople, intermarriage between the royal houses of England and France, and some six hundred years ahead of her time, the Vatican as a papal sovereign state. All these prophecies and many lesser ones were fulfilled exactly.

But there were entirely different kinds of Revelations of Birgitta which exercised a subtle and moulding influence over the religious and cultural mind of Europe. Visions of the Nativity and the Passion of Christ are two masterpieces of religious literature which can compare with the Bible and Dante's works. They were written at the time when the humanist Boccaccio wrote his Decameron, heralding neo-pagan Renaissance as a way of life. Birgitta had a vision of Our Lady, "Thou shalt come to the Holy City when so shall be the pleasure of my Son. From there thou shalt come to Bethlehem where I will show unto thee in every particular how it happened when I gave birth to my Son in this place." (Rev. VII, 1) Some thirty years later this vision of Mary was repeated and Birgitta then an old woman left for the pilgrimage to the Holy Land. Here over the silver star in the grotto of Bethlehem she could read "Hic de Vergine Maria Jesus Christus natus est," and Birgitta had a vision of the first Christmas night as follows.

"I saw an exceeding fair maiden who was with child. She was clad in a white cloak and a robe that was so thin that her virginal body could clearly be seen. Her body was very swollen for the womb was full and she was about to be delivered. With her there was a very honorable old man, and they had an ox and an ass with them. And when they were come into the cave the old man tied the ox and the ass to the manger, then he went out and came in again with a lighted taper, which he set fast between the stones in the wall, and went out again not to be present at the birth. Then the maid took off her shoes, laid aside the white cloak that she wore, likewise the veil that she had on her head and laid them by her side. She was now clad only in the robe, and her hair, that was bright like gold, fell down over her shoulders. She took out two small pieces of linen and two very fine woolen cloths that she had with her to wrap the child in and two other small pieces of woolen stuff to bind about its head, and she laid it all by her side until the time should come when she would use them. When all things were now ready the maiden knelt down with great awe and began to pray. She turned her back to the manger, but lifted her face towards heaven and looked to the East. And with hands uplifted and her eyes towards heaven she knelt without moving, as it were enrapt in divine sweetness. And while she was thus absorbed in prayer I saw that which was in her womb move and in a moment she gave birth to her Son. And so much light went out from Him that the taper which the old man had brought no longer gave any light. . . ."

"But so sudden and instant was the movement of the Infant that I could not see or distinguish how birth came to pass. I saw at once the child lying on the ground, naked but very clean. There was no dirt nor anything unclean upon it. And immediately the maiden's body, which had newly been very swollen, contracted and her whole body was wonderfully beautiful and delicate. But when the maiden felt that she was delivered she bent her head and folded her hands, and with great awe she adored the child and said to Him: 'Welcome, my God, my Lord, and my Son.' But then the boy wept and trembled with cold on the hard floor, and stretched out His little hands to His Mother, and she took Him up and laid His cheek against her and took Him to her breast with joy and great compassion. And she sat down on the floor and laid Him on her knees and began to swathe Him — first with the linen clothes and then with the woolen pieces and at last wound the whole about His little body, legs, and arms in one swaddling cloth, and swathed His head in the two woolen pieces that she had brought with her. When all this was done the old man came in and threw himself upon his knees, adoring the child and weeping for joy. And in the Virgin there was no weakness as in other women, when they are delivered, but she stood up with the child in her arms, and she and Joseph laid Him in the manger and adored Him with great joy. And then I heard wonderful sweet singing of many angels." (Rev. VII, 24)

Prince Orsini in his deposition at the canonization of Birgitta testified that in the Church of St. Anthony in Naples, he saw a painting in 1380 exactly in accord with the Revelations. It is known that Birgitta was venerated as a saint in Naples before she was canonized. Prince Orsini made a point in describing a new style in portraying the Nativity scene. The new style portrayed Mary in a white robe, kneeling in a devotional prayer, her hair falling over her shoulders, ineffable light radiating from her Son, angels singing as the words were spoken, "Welcome my God, my Lord and my Son". St. Joseph depicted either as entering with a candle into the manger, or praying with full reverence. This description of the Nativity scene by St. Birgitta, differed from the previous portrayals, where Our Lady was either sitting or reclining over the bed, her hair fully covered, Joseph sleeping in the corner of a cave and no rays of light shining from the Christ Child.

This type of portrayal came from Byzantine religious art and was prevalent in the middle of the XIV century. This so called "bourgeois realism" with all its trivialities and banalities and grossness was poor taste to Birgitta. She had been accustomed to St. Bernard's mystical religiosity which paid a great deal of attention to the Nativity and Passion of Christ and the Glories and Sorrows of Our Lady. Later this trend was cultivated by St. Francis and St. Bonaventura in the Franciscan school of piety. Birgitta grew up in this mystical, idealistic and tragic portrayal of the Holy Family, Apostles and Saints of the XIII century. Her tutors were the most educated clerics of her time in Sweden, and her friendship with the leading Roman aristocracy made her aware of religious art. For instance, as Prof. Henrik Cornell says, "to represent St. Joseph using his trousers to wrap the new born child with, because everything was missing, even swaddling clothes, — was to aristocratic and well educated Birgitta unacceptable." For Birgitta the Nativity of Christ was a major mystery where God chose the Word to become flesh in the human form in order to be better understood by the humanity. The birth of Christ was to her a supernatural event which needed, with all the spiritual beauty and nobility, to be put into harmony with the lines of sublime lyricism. Birgitta's Revelation came in the historical fulness of time and decided a new trend in portrayal of the Nativity for all subsequent centuries. Birgitta did not go into the XIII century tragic style, but refused to compromise with the so called realism of her own time. Instead she heralded a new spiritualized, supernaturalized idealism called "a great lyric period in art." It lasted in full glory from 1380 until 1430.

The enclosed reproductions, the fresco by the Lorenzetti School and the painting by Niccolo de Tommaso prove the point.

The Byzantine cave with the manger slowly disappeared in the art of Western Europe. Fra Angelico, Fra Lippi, Fabriano, Francke, Memling, Lochner, Altsdorfer, Dürer and Titian and Tintoretto all followed Birgitta's Revelations. Anton Wisher called himself "Birgitten Meister."

Academically the issue was raised about the historical background of Birgitta's Revelations on the Nativity. Divinely inspired Revelations are transcendental, and the frame of references in which they took place is secondary. Narratives of this kind enrich the sparse account of the Gospels and contribute to already existing tradition. Birgitta must have been aware of Pseudo-Bonaventura's Meditations which speak so much about the Nativity scene. Bonaventura belongs to the Franciscan school of piety so dear to Birgitta. However as Prof. Cornell says "the kneeling position of the Virgin in the Meditations is not so sanctified and supernatural as in Birgitta's Revelations, but considered as the position of an earthly woman while bearing." In Meditations the Virgin gets out of bed seeking support against a pillar (customary in biblical times) which does not imply a divine mystery of the painless Virgin birth. The words of Our Lady, "Bene veneris Deus meus, Dominus meus, et Filius meus," are original with Birgitta because they are not to be found in the Latin nor English version of Pseudo-Bonaventura's Meditations. A Birgittine monk, as a translator, put these words of Birgitta into Swedish translation of the Meditations.

St. Birgitta was often portrayed in the Nativity scene because artists wanted to acknowledge and compliment her Revelations as a source of inspiration. The only other saint often portrayed was St. Jerome because he lived for some thirty years in the grotto of Bethlehem translating the Bible. As Prof. Henrik Cornell concludes, St. Birgitta's Revelations had a major influence on the portrayal of the Nativity in the arts, sculpture, literature and music. In conclusion, it can be said that the Christmas story is better known and celebrated because of Birgitta's Revelations.

B. Puccini, XVIII C.   Rome

IMMACULATE CONCEPTION AND BIRGITTA

"That hour, therefore, in which I was conceived, may well be called a golden hour, for then began the salvation of mankind and darkness gave way to light."
(Rev. V, 13)

Lorenzetti School, XIV C.   S. Maria Novella, Florence

VISION OF BETHLEHEM

In her Book of Revelations, St. Birgitta describes her vision of Bethlehem in such a biblical style that it influenced the whole religious art. As a compliment, Birgitta was often portrayed in the Nativity scene. This fourteenth century fresco was damaged by the flood in 1966.

Niccolo di Tommaso, XIV C.   Pinacoteca Vaticana

"WELCOME, MY GOD, MY LORD AND MY SON."

These holy words are attributed to the Virgin Mary through the vision of the Nativity scene by St. Birgitta of Sweden, and represent an original contribution to the Church. This fourteenth century Florentine painting is the oldest of this kind.

Turino di Vanni, XIV C.   S. Matteo Museum, Pisa

THE FIRST CHRISTMAS NIGHT

The Sienese School entrenched in its medieval piety readily accepted St. Birgitta's Revelations in portraying the Nativity scene faithfully: "the stable in grotto ... watchful shepherds ... Virgin Mary in white ... St. Joseph with the candle etc ..."

Andreas Giltinger, XVI C.   Rosgarden Museum, Constance

THE HOLY FAMILY AND BIRGITTA

*In the religious art of the Nativity scene prior to Birgitta's Revelations, Our
Lady was portrayed either standing or reclining by the crib. After Birgitta's
vision, the Virgin Mary is always kneeling in full devotion and St. Joseph in
full reverence to the Holy Saviour.*

German Renaissance, XV C.   St. Kastor Church, Koblenz

ST. BIRGITTA'S MADONNA

In her Book of Revelations St. Birgitta showed a great love for the Christ Child and Our Lady. All Birgittine monasteries and convents were named after Mary. Therefore religious artists often portrayed St. Birgitta in an image of Our Lady.

Chapter VI

PASSION OF CHRIST

Frances T. Innis, XX C.   Santa Barbara

CHRIST IS MY SALVATION

Passion of Christ

When Birgitta wrote her Book of Revelations she assumed the stature of Moses, the fervor of St. Bernard, and the language of Dante. The spiritual impact of her Revelations was so great that literary critics speak of "Birgitta as the most powerful figure Sweden ever had," of her Vision of the Nativity as "admirable poetry of a sublime lyricism which unveils the visions of Jerusalem," and of her description of the Passion of Christ as "authentic poetry with a biblical flavor." Her reliving of the Passion of Christ at Golgotha led to the adoration of The Five Wounds of Christ, and to The Fifteen Orations to Jesus called "Fifteen, Oh Jesus" prayers which comforted the persecuted in XVI century Europe. The Glories and Sorrows of Our Lady led to the Birgittine Rosary. The great German romanticist Clemens Brentano, in his work "Sufferings of Christ" felt that Birgitta's Revelations amplified the New Testament and served as the greatest inspiration to the Western World.

The Blessed Virgin herself revealed to Birgitta with the tenderness of a Mother to a mother, that while on earth, there was not an hour in which grief did not pierce her soul. "As often I looked at my Son, as often as wrapped Him in His swaddling clothes, as often as I saw His hands and feet, so often was my soul absorbed in fresh grief, for I thought how He would be crucified." The afflicted Mother already knew from the prophecy of the Old Testament that her Son was to suffer. "When suckling Him she thought of the gall and vinegar, when swathing Him of the cords with which He was to be bound, when bearing Him in her arms of the Cross to which He was to be nailed, when sleeping of His death." That sword of sorrow was every hour approaching nearer to the Blessed Virgin, as the time for the Passion of her Son drew nearer. And Our Lady of Sorrows concludes to Birgitta: "Then He was taken to the pillar of torment, and He took off His vestment Himself, and He laid His hands upon the pillar Himself, and His enemies bound them fast without mercy."

"And as He stood there bound to the pillar He had no garments on at all, but was as naked as when He had come into the world and suffered shame that He had to endure this. Then all my Son's friends fled from Him, and His enemies surrounded Him and tore His body that was so pure and without blemish, and without any infection or sin. But I, who was standing near, fell down like one dead at one sound of the first blow. And when I came to myself I saw His body beaten and torn, so that the ribs could be seen. And what was still more dreadful to see was that when the scourges were withdrawn His flesh was torn like the earth by a plough. And as my Son was now standing there, bleeding and wounded all over, so that there was not a whole spot left upon Him, there was one who took courage and asked: 'Will you kill Him, though He is not yet judged?' They then clothed my Son in His garments, and I saw there was blood in all the places where He had trod. And the executioners did not allow Him to put on all His garments but pushed and pulled Him, telling Him to hasten. He was taken away like a robber and He dried the blood from His eyes."

"But on the way to the place of torment some struck Him on the neck, some in the face, and the blows were so hard that, although I could not see anything for the people, I could hear the sound of the blows. And when I came to the place of torment I saw everything made ready for His death."

Our Lady described to Birgitta the Crucifixion "where the bone on the hand was hardest and firmest" and of the Crown of Thorns: "It pricked so hard that both my Son's eyes were filled with the blood that flowed down, and the ears were stopped up and His beard was thick with blood. And as He now stood there, so ill-used, bleeding and pierced, He saw me, standing there and weeping, and with His eyes full of blood, He looked at my sister's son, John, and gave me into his care. And I heard some say that my Son was a robber, and others said that He was a deceiver, and that no one had deserved His punishment better than He. And hearing all this made me still more sorrowful. But when I heard the blow of the last nail being struck it grew dark before my eyes, my hands and feet shook and I fell to the ground like one dead."

"But when I rose again I saw my Son hanging there so miserably, and I, His Sorrowful Mother, could hardly stand up, and when He saw me He cried to His Father with a loud and tearful voice and said: 'Father, why hast Thou forsaken Me?' Then His eyes looked as if they were already dim, His cheeks were hollow, the mouth was open, His tongue was bleeding, His stomach was flat against His back, as if He had no entrails, His whole body white from the great loss of blood, His hands and feet were stretched out hard, and the nails had made them as it were cross-shaped, His beard and hair were all full of blood. So did my Son stand on the Cross, wounded and bleeding, only His heart was sound, for it was the best and strongest nature, for from my flesh He had taken the very purest body. His skin was so fine that even the slightest scratch made the blood come, and the veins could be seen through the skin. And because His nature was of the very best, life and death strove a long while in His wounded body. For sometimes the pains from His torn body went up to the heart, which was the strongest part of Him, and sometimes the pains again darted into the limbs, and the death agony was long and bitter. And as my Son was suffering thus He looked down at His weeping friends who would rather have endured all His agony or burn forever in hell, than see Him thus in agony. And the sorrow over the sorrow of His friends was more than all the other suffering in either His limbs or His heart, for He loved them exceedingly. But now when His fear and torment was becoming greater than He could endure, He cried to His Father and said: 'Father, into Thy hands I commend My spirit.' And when I, His Mother, heard this cry, all my limbs trembled in my heart's bitterest need, and afterwards, every time I thought of it, it was as if I heard those words again. But now, when death came, and His heart broke, all His limbs trembled, and His head rose up a little and then bowed down again. His mouth was open, His tongue full of blood, His fingers and arms shrank a little. His back fell hard on the Cross. Then someone said to me: 'Mary, your Son is dead.' Others said: 'He is dead but He shall surely rise from the dead.' Then they all went away, but one came and thrust a spear into His side. And when the spear was drawn out, the point was red with blood, and it was to me as if my own heart was cut assunder. Thereafter He was taken down from the Cross, and I laid Him over my knees, and He looked like a leper. His eyes were glazed and full of blood, His mouth cold as snow, His beard like grass, His face shrunken, His arms had grown so stiff that they could not bend farther down than to the navel. As He hung on the Cross, so I had Him upon my knees, and He was like a man who is crippled in all His limbs. Then they laid Him in a clean linen shroud, and I closed His eyes and His mouth, for they were open. After that they laid Him in the sepulchre. Oh, my daughter, how willingly would I not have gone into the grave with Him, if this had been His will. When this was done the good John came and took me home. Behind us we left the Cross standing high and alone." (Rev. VI, 57-58)

As Birgitta knelt at Golgotha, the ultimate dream of every Christian pilgrim, she could remember the first vision of Christ in far away Sweden. Here as an old woman of seventy, Birgitta reconstructed the scene of the Sorrowful Mother under the Cross: "And now, as I looked at all this cruelty, overwhelmed with grief, I saw His Sorrowful Mother, trembling and half dead, and her sisters and John comforting her, and they stood not far from the Cross on its right side. And then a new pain pierced me, and it was as though I was pierced with an exceeding bitter sword. At length she rose, the Sorrowful Mother, and looked up at her Son, and her sisters held her up, and she stood there like one living dead, pierced with the sword of grief. And when her Son saw her and the other friends standing and weeping, He commended her in a wailing voice to John. And it was plain to be seen from His bearing and to be heard from His voice that His heart was pierced with compassion for His Mother with the sharpest dart of grief." (Rev. V, 15)

Birgitta felt the grief with the heart of Our Lady. But for Birgitta, Golgotha was fulfillment of her mystical love of Our Lady and Our Lord, and only a few months later Birgitta reached the end of her earthly pilgrimage. Reading Birgitta's Passion of Our Lord and seeing the famous masterpieces of art, especially the Crucifixion by Matthias Grünewald, where one can notice every drop of blood down the cheeks of Christ in the agony of death, one can understand how the Book of Revelations and the arts are intimately related. Grünewald as a German Renaissance Master of the XVI century could not portray the Crucifixion merely on the fragmentary Gospels. It took this grand and tragic approach of Birgitta to inspire the centuries in all the arts. Emperor Maximilian I of the Holy Roman Empire understood the importance of the Book of Revelations and insisted on several editions. Imperial Nuremberg became the cultural center of Renaissance Germany which thrived on the heritage of Birgitta's Revelations. To Maximilian I, himself a man of letters, "one illustrated edition of the Book of Revelations by St. Birgitta was worth more, than all marble edifices." Under the influence of the Revelations a new wave of Christian piety spread all over Europe, especially in the social and cultural centers as Florence and Nuremberg, and in the capitals as Rome, London, Paris, Madrid, Brussells, Stockholm and Vienna.

L. Schäufelin, XVI C.   Nuremberg

BIRGITTA ATTENDING THE WOUNDS

The dream of every Christian is to undertake a pilgrimage to Jerusalem. To climb the steep road to Golgotha and to relive the Passion of Christ, where almost two thousand years ago the hammer strokes over the Cross started Christian civilization. Woe to Western man if these strokes do not resound in his ears anymore!

German Renaissance, XV C.   Nuremberg

FRIENDS OF GOD AT GOLGOTHA

The Prior Peter of Alvastra played the major role in the life of St. Birgitta by translating the Revelations into Latin, and taking part in her canonization. He followed Birgitta everywhere until the last moment of her life.

Italian Baroque, XVIII C.　　　　　　St. Mary's Church, Florence

BISHOP ALPHONSE AT GOLGOTHA

Bishop Alphonse of Jaen played a decisive role in the life of St. Birgitta as her confessor and official translator of the Revelations into curial Latin. After her death Bishop Alphonse lived as a hermit in Genoa.

Paolo Vetri, XX C.   St. Birgitta Church, Naples

VISION OF THE CROSS

Birgitta, a true Tertiary of St. Francis, carried her Cross throughout her life with a prayerful patience. Her Saintliness became so great that her mere presence could have led sinners to conversion, or the sick a miraculous healing.

G. Farelli, XVII C.   St. Birgitta Church, Naples

VISION OF FIVE WOUNDS

Birgitta showed such great love and devotion to Our Lord Crucified that in Franciscan prayers one can hear Christ saying to her: "If I had not created the world already, I would have created it for you, Birgitta."

B. Puccini, XVIII C.   Domus Birgittae, Rome

IN QUEST OF THE HOLY GRAIL

"My Lord Jesus, You are a Divine Knight who led the people out of darkness of suffering into eternal joy, because with the blood of Your heart, You opened Paradise for mankind."

(Prayer of St. Birgitta)

Chapter VII

THE KNIGHTHOOD OF ST. BIRGITTA

Italian Baroque, XVIII C.   St. Birgitta Church, Naples

PATRONESS OF KNIGHTS

The Knighthood of St. Birgitta

Except for St. Bernard, no saint exceeded Birgitta in writing on Christian chivalry as opposed to the secular chivalry, which she used to call "the chivalry of the devil." She wrote some hundred pages about Knighthood, its structure, purposes, ceremonies and attire. Her religious and knightly friends, who dedicated themselves to carrying the Gospel as missionaries and warriors for Christ, she often called "friends of God."

The failure of the Crusades of her cousin King Magnus Eriksson in Finland and the superbia of the Teutonic knights made Birgitta very critical of the secular chivalry, or rather Christian chivalry which became secularized. Her warning against the decadence of the Christian Knighthood are masterpieces of literature in the Middle Ages. St. Birgitta, already being a patroness of the Christian nobility through her family relations with many European courts, because of her definite stand on Knighthood, became sort of a high protectoress of all knightly orders. She appears as a kind but firm mother to her knightly children.

Historians of the Religious and Military Orders of Chivalry all concur that St. Birgitta of Sweden, together with the Religious Order of the Most Holy Saviour, instituted a Military and Chivalric Order. Whereas the religious order was conceived as a missionary order to expand Christianity into barbarian lands and to regenerate the faith in already Catholic countries, the chivalric order was conceived as a complement to the establishment of monasteries, hospitals, hospices and orphanages. This idea grew out of St. Birgitta's own experience in the XIV century when the landed aristocracy joined the monasteries by leaving all their possessions to the Church. St. Birgitta's idea was that the Catholic elite of the country should in their old age think about preparing themselves for heaven by endowing the Church with lands. All Birgittine monasteries were founded in this way by Kings and Princes and by the elite of the country, as St. Birgitta insisted. Some of the historians of St. Birgitta's Military Order assert that the Order was primarily founded as a fighting order to defend the Baltic countries from the intrusion of

73

the heathen barbarians. Chronologically that would mean that the Order took part of the Livonian Order of the Sword, and of the Order of Saint Mary known as the Teutonic Order. St. Birgitta favored the Swedish crusade of her cousin King Magnus to the Baltic lands, and her own brother Israel found his death fighting as a Knight. Later in Rome, St. Birgitta favored the Crusade against the Turks in the Levant and in the Balkans. Many crusading leaders such as Cardinal Cesarini or Marshal Boucicaut or the great Father Capistrano fought against the Turks in the spirit of St. Birgitta. The heresies of John Wycliff and John Huss were fought equally with the Birgittine fervor of preserving the faith. Emperor Sigismund a leader in this combating of the heresies was a High Protector of the Birgittines. In short, the Birgittine Order was a social force among the nobility, and a military force to defend the faith against the heretics and the barbarians.

A French historian J. Hermant, in his volume, "The History of the Orders of Chivalry," speaks with authority about the Birgittine chivalric order at the times when barbarians intruded into Poland, Sweden, Denmark and the Baltic lands. Hermant says that St. Birgitta, a Swedish princess instituted a military order in 1366 with the purpose of combating the invasion of the heathens, to limit the heretics in their expansion, and to take care of widows, orphans and the aged. The Birgittine Knightly Order took as an emblem a blue maltese cross with the symbolic fire underneath of the Cross. The Blue Cross stood for the immense love of the Church, and the fire symbolized the ardor of the faith. The Order of St. Birgitta was based on the Augustinian rule and recognized by Pope Urban V in 1370. The standard of the Order had a Cross on one side and three royal crowns of the Goths on the other. Another prominent historian, Michele y Marquez, adds that the forms of arming the knights, the benedictions and the profession of the knights, followed the pontifical of the Order of St. John, known today as Malta. The knights advanced according to their seniority, thereby giving opportunity to a young knight of becoming a Grand Master of the Order. The Order persisted until the Protestant revolution in 1599 in Sweden and then moved out of the country into Poland, Germany, France, Spain and Italy.

Dahlberg, in his Suecia Antiqua e Moderna, speaks of the Birgittine chivalric order flourishing in Sweden about 1396, at the time when St. Birgitta was proclaimed a national patron saint of Sweden by the great Queen Margareth. Her successor, King Erik XIII, a devoted Birgittine, was knighted together with some thirty-six knights. The recent Royal Book of the Swedish Orders speak about the Knightly Order of St. Birgitta as established by Queen Margareth in honor of her favored Saint Birgitta and furnished it with rich commendas. For instance, Governor Petersson of Ulfasa and Governor Magnusson of Finsta received the Knighthood of St. Birgitta ("Riddare of Sta. Brita") in 1396 from the hands of Queen Margareth for their merits to their country. It appears clearly that the Queen used the Birgittine Cross as a royal decoration of merit. Another historian, Jonas Bång, cites the names of Pavel Mansson Bjug and his descendants of the famous family of Ulf-spårre who received the Knighthood of St. Birgitta in 1447 for their generous assistance to the monastery of Vadstena. The Ulfspårre family had many daughters in the convent of Vadstena, some being prioresses and related to the family of St. Birgitta. It proves that the knights and ladies supported the monasteries in abundance. The great French poetess in the XIV century Christine de Pisan, speaks of a well known troubadour, Othon F. Guillaume de Grand Son, in 1397, saying that his literary fame disappeared before his glory as a brillant knight of the Most Holy Saviour, popularly known as the Order of St. Birgitta. A. G. Horn, in his historical sketch on knightly orders, speaks in 1768 about the Catholic Knightly Order of St. Birgitta for the Swedish Catholic aristocracy. In appendix, article VII, it says that the Abbess General of the Birgittines in Rome was functioning as a grand master of the order.

Just as in the XIV century encroaching humanism tried to undermine Christianity with the revived Greco-Roman pagan classicism, similarly in the XIX century encroaching liberalism with its atheistic and secular overtones, linked with the power politics in Italy and Europe, tried to destroy the Church. At the time of 1366, when Europe expected the birth of another Lucifer, the Military Order of St. Birgitta saw its light. Equally in the XIX century the Southern Italian aristocracy, as their forefathers who feted Birgitta in Naples, arose all over Italy in defense of the Church by reviving the traditional Birgittine Military Order. Some hundred princely families of Southern Italy and some from Florence, Genoa, Bologna and Rome came together and with the advice of the noble Cardinal Giuseppe de Cosenza of Naples, one of the oldest archbishoprics in the Church, and with the approval of the chivalric King Francis II of Bourbons of Both Sicilies convened three consecutive assemblies in the symbolic Church of the Holy Saviour, in order to reconstitute the Order. Among the leading families present were the Commenos, Pierangeli, Pignatelli, Caraffa, Caracciolo, Paterno, San Severino etc. Naples, being the largest city in Italy and the capital of the Kingdom of Both Sicilies, lent a great deal of prestige to the Order. Commander Fenicia in his historical sketch, gives a complete picture of the reconstitution of the Order in 1859 under the Grand Mastership of Count Vincenzo Abbate de Castello Orleans, Sr.

With the coming of the House of Savoy to power in 1861 many Orders from the time of the Bourbons were abolished, but the Birgittine Knightly Order survived. When the Republic of Italy was proclaimed in 1946 by replacing the House of Savoy, again many Orders were abolished but the Birgittine survived against all expectations.

In 1959, a hundred years after the reconstitution of the Order, the Supreme Court of Italy brought a decision about the nature and legal position of the Order, declaring it a "Non-national and Independent Order".

Today's Order of the Knights of St. Birgitta is following in the footsteps of the traditional "Equites Briccianes," taking care of charities as monasteries and orphanages, furthering Christian culture, and expanding the Ecumenical movement toward Christian unity. Today the Order is numerically one of the strongest, and because of its Ecumenical tendencies, the most contemporary. The seat of the Order is Naples, Italy. The Grand Mastership of the Order is hereditary in the House of the family of Counts Vincenzo Abbate de Castello Orléans, Sr.

St. Birgitta gave a message to the world that is as modern today as it was in her century. She is the only female saint who has her Military-Knightly Order flourishing in the world. The official Church rejoices in every good deed the Order performs, yet regrets any failure. In these trying times, when the Church is in similar dangers as it was in the XIV and XIX centuries, the Religious and the Knightly Orders of St. Birgitta are trying to answer the challenges of their time in defense of the Mother Church.

VISION OF ST. MICHAEL ARCHANGEL

In grand Christian tradition, St. Michael symbolized the supreme virtues of a Knight, in obedience to the Mother Church, defense against the forces of evil, protection of the weak and charity towards the poor. To St. Birgitta Archangel Michael served as a model Knight.

Buonani, S. J. XVII C.   Ordini militari

CHEVALIER DE ST. BIRGITTA

"The Military Order of St. Birgitta was instituted by Birgitta, Princess of Sweden, in 1366 under the Pontificate of Pope Urban V, who approved the Order by giving it the Augustinian rule. The ensign of the Order is the blue Malta Cross with a tongue of fire as a symbol of the ardor of Faith."

(Encyclopédie Catholique, Paris 1842)

Dahlberg, XVIII C.   Suecia antiqua

MILITARY AND KNIGHTLY ORDERS OF SWEDEN

1. *Order of Seraphim in XIV C.*
2. *Order of the Baltic Sword, XIII C.*
3. *Order of St. Birgitta in XIV C.*
4. *Order of the Holy Saviour, XVI C.*
5. *Order of the Agnus Dei in XVI C.*
6. *Order of the Amarante, XVII C.*

Knightly ceremony   St. Birgitta Church, Naples

AUTHOR'S INVESTITURE INTO THE ORDER

The Order of St. Birgitta was reconstituted in 1859 under the leadership of the Count Vincent Abbate de Castello Orléans, Sr. — spiritual advice of the noble Cardinal Giuseppe de Cosenza of Naples, and approved by the King Francis II of both Sicilies. In 1959 the Supreme Court of Italy declared the Order an Independent and Non-National Order.

Ecumenical dialogue   Vatican City, 1966

FOR THE CAUSE OF CHRIST AND UNITY

His Holiness Pope Paul VI received the world famous tenor Lauritz Melchior in a private audience. Lauritz, a prominent Lutheran, received the Grand Cross of Saint Birgitta in a religious-knightly ceremony in Naples. The President of the Supreme Court of Italy, His Excellency Dr. Ernesto Eula served as his knightly God-father.

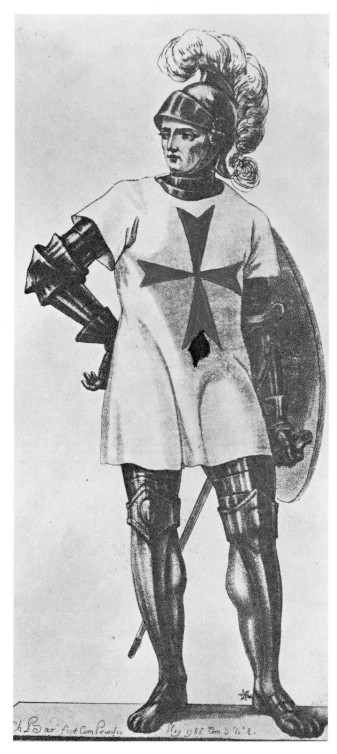

KNIGHT OF ST. BIRGITTA

"A Knight of Honour is he who strives with all his might to give glory to God and he who is ready to suffer for God's sake. He is God's Knight and will be made Knight in Heaven." (Rev. IV, 55)

Chapter VIII

IN THE FOOTSTEPS OF ST. BIRGITTA

Skederid Church, XV C.   Uppland

A LEADER OF MEN

In the Footsteps of St. Birgitta

A few years ago in beautiful Vienna the author was visiting the father of his friend, a distinguished gentleman of the old school, an aristocrat and a cavalry officer of the Imperial and Royal Austro-Hungarian army. In his palatial home there was a private chapel with a painting of Christ Crucified by Guido Reni at the altar. On the marble step there was a parchment with a neatly handwritten "Fifteen, Oh Jesus" prayers by St. Birgitta of Sweden. The most fascinating conversation followed in which the old gentleman touched upon his youthful and happy life in Imperial Vienna, a life of "Wine, women and song," and now a life of dignity, and prayerful repentance to St. Birgitta. He made an almost hesitant remark, "St. Birgitta is (or better, she was) a patron saint of aristocracy which jealously carried her in its heart as an almost private saint. To me, Birgitta is my sponsor with Christ Whom I, as a sinner, have offended." This remark led to the following research.

Birgitta was very firm with her children. Regardless of what anyone thinks of "Birgitta's stick," used on her daughter Catherine, the fact is that Catherine turned out to be a saint. In a formative age children must be guided for their best. Another Catherine of Siena under the influence of Bishop Alphonse and Niccolo Soderini, both friends of St. Birgitta, followed in her footsteps in bringing the Pope back to Rome. Even Joan of Arc, who changed the course of the history of France was very much aware of St. Birgitta. Prince Niccolo Orsini served as a messenger of Birgitta to Popes Urban V and Gregory XI to Avignon. It took a real faith in Birgitta to dare to transmit the menacing parchments to the Popes. Cardinal Sabran who met Birgitta as a young man followed her holy advice and became a great man of the Church. Later he participated in the canonization of St. Birgitta. Pope Urban V repented to Birgitta, and Gregory XI after her last admonition returned to Rome. Pope Urban VI had a portrait of Birgitta on his desk and always quoted Birgitta's Revelations to make a point in difficult times. Pope John XXIII, later anti-pope, in his old age repented his sins by praying to Birgitta. Pope

Boniface IX, a great devotee of Birgitta, happily canonized her as a saint. Pope Martin V of the house of Colonna, which loved Birgitta, reconfirmed the canonization. Cardinals Orsini, Cesarini, Torquemada, and Panormitanus took a stand in the Councils of Constance and Basel in favor of Birgitta, defending her Revelations against the French Cardinal Gerson, who "because of Avignon policy," attacked Birgitta. Chivalric King Henry V of England, Emperor Sigismund of the Holy Roman Empire, and King Erik XIII of Sweden greatly admired and loved St. Birgitta. Henry V even married because of Birgitta's prophecy, Sigismund became the High Protector of the Birgittines in Europe and fought the heretics in the name of St. Birgitta. Erik XIII went to far away Jerusalem as a humble pilgrim in the name of Birgitta. Great Queen Margareth of Sweden, Norway, and Denmark built monasteries in the name of Birgitta, and Queen Phillipa of Sweden had only one wish: to be buried close to St. Birgitta. Emperor Charles IV of the Holy Roman Empire, while visiting Rome, listened humbly to the words of Birgitta on Humility, Abstinence, Self-denial and Charity. Emperor John Paleologus of the Eastern Roman Empire was deeply impressed with Birgittas call for Christian unity. Emperor Maximilian I of the Holy Roman Empire, "the last knight", read the Revelations second to the Bible, and Queen Christine of Sweden returned to the Mother Church in the name of Birgitta. Emperor Ferdinand III of Austria-Hungary was a great devotee of St. Birgitta and, after his victory over the Swedes, built a beautiful Chapel outside of Vienna in her honour. The great saints, theologians and cardinals wrote about St. Birgitta with devout admiration, St. Clara of Pisa, St. Antoninus of Florence, St. Aloysius of Naples, St. Peter Canisius, St. Robert Bellarmine, Surius, Blosius, Bollandus, Baronius, Pole, Newman, etc. Columbus, born in the shadow of the Birgittine monastery "Scala Coeli Mariae et Birgittae," was her great devotee. St. Thomas More read her Revelations and often visited the Birgittine monastery at Syon. The masters Tommaso, Fra Angelico, Fra Lippi, Fra Bartolomeo, Grünewald, Dürer, Wisher, and Titian followed her Revelations. Universities at Oxford and Sorbonne, Vienna, Prague and Bratislava, and Princeton studied Revelations. Emperor Maximilian II of Mexico had Birgitta's portrait in his private chambers, and Pope Pius XI on his working desk.

The fundamental question arises, "Why were all these and many other leaders fascinated with St. Birgitta?" Why today, when hardly anybody speaks of saints, is St. Birgitta the most interesting saint?

Birgitta's life was so saintly, so dedicated to Christ and His Church that she served as an inspiring example. She was convinced that she was God's instrument. Some two hundred miracles speak about her strength of faith. This conviction was so deep that hardly anybody could resist her. Her Revelations proved to be right and were fulfilled as she prophesied them. Her greatness attracted greatness.

Her absolute sincerity about reforming the decadent Christian Knighthood made her a sort of mother protectoress of Knighthood. As Dawson said "Knighthood never lost its appeal to the Western world," because it epitomized the highest aspirations of a true man and a gentleman. Nostalgia for the romantic ages persists even until today regardless of the rhythm of modern technology. The virtues of a Knight, to stand by His Church, to enoble life, and to protect the weak and poor are perennial virtues. Birgitta upheld these virtues, and one can say that a true Knight is a Knight of St. Birgitta regardless of the Order to which he belongs.

Birgitta traveled all over Europe as a pilgrim. Many saints and kings traveled to many shrines, Birgitta visited all of them. Therefore she is considered a patron saint of pilgrims.

In Sweden and Italy there is a legend that eight days before a person is supposed to die, St. Birgitta comes to comfort him and prepare for a gentle death. Such a belief is a great consolation in facing the painful thought of death. In Italy there are many such stories and poems in honour of Birgitta.

There is a general appeal of St. Birgitta for Knights, for pilgrims and for persons approaching death. Birgitta appears to be an answer to many for many reasons. Above all, she appeals to social leadership because Birgitta was a true leader herself. To pray to St. Birgitta for intercession with Christ means to be forgiven. To pray to St. Birgitta for intercession with Our Lady means to be loved again.

Birgitta fits excellently into the world of tomorrow. Modern technology as a synthesis of man's aspiration, and knowledge will lead into outer space. The forms of our way of life will continue to change, but the problem of the human soul will be eternal. Rich or poor, sick or healthy, on this earth or another planet, there will be the same yearning of the human soul after God. That was the attitude of St. Birgitta.

The brave new world of tomorrow will be an overcrowded, over-mechanized and over-polluted human beehive with plenty of leisure, and search after pleasures, culture and God. Many institutions of yesterday will not be able to perform their functions and will disappear. The Church and the priesthood will be like a torch in the darkness, similar to the Dark Ages when the Benedictine Abbeys were the only light in the wilderness. In the new technological and materialistic age, which will yearn after spirit, the Church will lead and educate through mass communications such as radio and television. Individual soul and conscience hidden in its beehive cell will yearn to communicate with God.

The future belongs to Ecumenism. By the existing division Christianity is crucified. For the love of Christ there will be One Shepherd and one flock. St. Birgitta, in the XIV century, was urging the Greeks to return to the rock of the Church. St. Birgitta, although a Catholic saint, is understood by her Christian brethern today, and will be understood by all the people of God tomorrow.

Woodcut, XV C.   Lübeck, Germany

PATRONESS OF THE CHRISTIAN NOBILITY

In the times of feudal Europe, St. Birgitta was considered the patroness of Christian nobility. Today she is considered a patroness of social leadership, no longer nobility of blood, but nobility of spirit.

Andrea Vaccari, XVI C.   Royal Palace, Naples

ST. CATHERINE OF SIENA

St. Catherine of Siena, a Dominican Tertiary and a Patron Saint of Italy
followed in the footsteps of St. Birgitta in bringing the Pope Gregory XI from
Avignon back to Rome.

Atilio Palombi, XIX C.   Domus Birgittae, Rome

ST. CATHERINE OF SWEDEN

St. Catherine followed in the footsteps of her saintly mother, and was elected the first Abbess of the monastery of Vadstena. She wrote "The consolation of the soul" and was canonized in 1484 by Pope Innocent VIII.

H. W. Bissen, XIX C.   Copenhagen

QUEEN MARGARETH

Queen Margareth of Sweden, Norway and Denmark was a great devotee of St. Birgitta. In 1396 Queen Margareth convened a National Council at Arbog and proclaimed St. Birgitta the patron saint of Sweden.

H. W. Bissen, XIX C.   Copenhagen

QUEEN PHILIPPA

Queen Philippa of Sweden followed the footsteps of St. Birgitta throughout her life, building churches, monasteries, hospitals and hospices in honour of Our Lord.

Albert Dürer, XVI C.   Vienna

EMPEROR MAXIMILIAN I.

The Emperor of the Holy Roman Empire, Maximilian I, was a great devotee of St. Birgitta. Second to the Bible, St. Birgitta's Revelations were his favored reading. During his reign the Revelations were published in his Imperial City of Nuremberg.

R. Werner, XX C.   Stockholm

QUEEN CHRISTINE

When Queen Christine of Sweden abdicated her throne and left for Rome to become a Catholic, she symbolically abdicated her crown to St. Birgitta. In Rome she stayed at the same palace where St. Birgitta had lived centuries before.

Henry Lefort, XIX C.   Madrid

CHRISTOPHER COLUMBUS

Genoa was a spiritual stronghold of St. Birgitta. Her monastery "The Heavenly Path of Mary and Birgittae" was called Conventus Angelicus, because it led more souls to God than all other monasteries in the city. Born in Genoa, Columbus often climbed the steep Path to the Convent in deep devotion to the Passion of Christ.

Hans Holbein, XVI C.   London

SIR THOMAS MORE

The Cult of St. Birgitta in XV century England prepared a spiritual atmosphere into which Sir Thomas More was born. He often visited the largest monastery in England "The Immaculate Conception and St. Birgitta." Birgitta, Columbus and Thomas More were Tertiaries of St. Francis and devotees to the Passion of Christ.

Cathedral, XIV C.   Uppsala

THE ECUMENICAL ST. BIRGITTA

St. Birgitta is the bridge between Catholic Rome and Protestant Sweden . . .
Scandinavia, nay the World.

Cardinal Eugene Tisserant, 1968

ANIMA EROICA

The plague reared up like a fiery horse
        and galloped through country and town.
Black, virile death rode with it —
        trampling Europe down.
War, war, war —
        that first-heard cannons' roar.
Revolts, the French and English,
        the Turks. War after war.
All virtue was choked, the damned went to hell,
And the good to desolate night.
The world was a forest, a wild, dark forest,
And the candle no longer burned bright.

O what did you want from this worldly life,
Be you prince or priest or a poor peasant's wife?

To have some money; to live well, my friend;
To be honored, esteemed; a fine show at the end.

The candle burned low in the window alone,
And few people cared how dimly it shone.

Stupor et mirabilia audita sunt in terra nostra.
Strange things have been heard in our land,
But none more strange than the still small voice
From the cloud above Birgitta's shoulder
That told her:

Thou shalt be my bride. My friends resemble birds.
They fly from bush to bush, ashamed to serve me,
Deaf to my words.
Through thee I will speak to the world.
Go to the sick, go to the poor,
Go to the king, go to the shrine.
I will guide you, my bride, my pilgrim.
Thou art mine.

In revelations she foresaw the marriage
That would end the war.
She saw the popes return to Rome,
The straits fall to the Turks,
The Vatican become the Church's home.
She saw reforms and unity
And knew she would not fail.
She saw her spirit win;
She saw her Christ prevail.

Angel of Rome and Mystic of the North,
Call us forth
As holy knights,
And knights are dear unto His sight,
As noble knights
Who rouse to action for the right,
Who strive in the present age
To save our heritage,
Each one an anima eroica,
Like you an anima eroica,
A united heroic spirit that would
Transform the world through love and brotherhood.

MERRILL SPARKS

BIBLIOGRAPHY
The Religious and Knightly Order of St. Birgitta

Adalsten, K., Licht aus dem Norden, Fribourg, 1951

Adlerfeldt, G., De Ordinibus equestribus, Stockholm, 1696

Anrep, G., Svenska adelns ättar-taflor, Stockholm, 1864

Antoninus, St., Chronica Antonini, Lugduni, 1543

Ashmole, E., The Institution, Laws and Ceremonies, London, 1672

Ballerini, R., S. Brigida, Roma, 1895

Bång, J., Ulfspårre Ätten, Stockholm, 1741

Bar, M., Ordres Religieux et Militaires, Paris, 1756

Binet, E., La vie de Ste Brigitte, Lille, 1634

Bisogni, E., La sacra e nobile Milizia, Roma, 1950

Buonani, F., Ordini religiosi e militari, Venezia, 1697

Burlamacchi, Vita di S. Brigida di Svezia, Napoli, 1692

Butkovich, A., Anima Eroica, Los Angeles, 1968

Cahier, Ch., Caracteristiques des Saints, Paris, 1867

Cento, E., All'ombra della Croce, Roma, 1959

Chiminelli, P., La Mistica del Nord, Roma, 1948

Clark, H., A concise history of Knighthood, London, 1794

Cnattingius, H., Studies in the Order of St. Bridget, Uppsala, 1963

Collijn, J., Iconographia Brigittina, Stockholm, 1918

Cornell, H., The Iconography of the Nativity, Stockholm, 1924

Coronelli, A., Ordinum Equestrum ac Militarum, Venezia, 1715

Crollalanza, Enciclopedia araldica cavallerescha, Roma, 1877

Cuomo, R., Ordini cavallereschi, Roma, 1780

Dahlberg, E., Suecia antiqua e hodierna, Stockholm, 1690

Dictionnaire des dictionnaires, Paris, 1889

Ekwall, S., Birgittavita, Stockholm, 1965

Encyclopédie Catholique, Paris, 1842

Fenicia, C., Milizia sacra di S. Brigida, Napoli, 1862

Ferraironi, F., Il Santuario di S. Brigida in Napoli, Roma, 1934

Flavigny, de., Sainte Brigitte de Suede, Paris, 1910

Fogelklou, E., S. Birgitta, Stockholm, 1919

Fogelklou, E., Bortom Birgittae, Stockholm, 1941

Frederici, A.M.O., Diplomatarium Nobilium, Villenoy, 1913

Genouillac, de., Dictionnaire de Chevalérie, Paris, 1891

Gersonius, J., De Theologia Mystica, Cologne, 1483

Gesta Gothorum, Gothstadt, 1940

Giustiniano, B., Ordini militari e cavallereschi, Venezia, 1672

Graf, D., Revelations and prayers of St. Bridget, London, 1928
Grisar, H., La casa di S. Brigida, Roma, 1895
Gryphius, C., Welt und Geistes Ritter-Orden, Leipzig, 1709
Hamilton, A., The angel of Syon, London, 1905
Hermant, J., Histoire des Ordres de Chevalerie, Rouen, 1692
Hoving, J., Gothic Golden Griffin Order, Gothstadt, 1939
Horn, G., Commilitiones Christi, Stockholm, 1937
Jean, C., St. Brigitte de Suede, Paris, 1890
Jorgenson, J., Saint Bridget of Sweden, New York, 1954
Lindblom, A., Life of St. Birgitta, Stockholm, 1908
Lindblom, A., Den heliga Birgittas Bilderwerk, Stockholm, 1918
Lobkowitz, J., Theologia regularis, Lyon, 1665
Löfström, K., Sweriges Riddarordnar, Stockholm, 1948
Magnino, B., S. Brigida di Swezia, Roma, 1939
Maigne, W., Les Ordres de Chevalerie, Paris, 1891
Mancini, A., S. Brigida di Svezia, Milano, 1960
Marquez, M. J., Cavalleria antiqua e moderna, Madrid, 1642
Mendo, A., De Ordinibus militaribus, Madrid, 1671
Mollat, G., Les Papes d'Avignon, Paris, 1949
Moroni, G., Dizionario storico-ecclesiastico, Venezia, 1840
Nyberg, T., Birgittinische Klostergründungen, Leiden, 1965
Olaus Magnus, Vita Catharinae, Roma, 1550
On. de Santa Maria, La cavalleria antica e moderna, Brescia, 1751
Oquendo, M., Vida di S. Brigida, San Sebastian, 1636
Paraiso, V., St. Bridget of Sweden, London, 1922
Peacey, E., Saint Birgitta of Sweden, London, 1933
Perrella, G., I Luoghi Santi, Piacenza, 1936
Perrot, A., Collection historique, Paris, 1820
Pourrat, P., Spiritualité chretienne, Paris, 1924
Potthast, A., Bibliotheca Historica Medii Aevi, Berlin, 1896
Ravaldi, N., Translation S. Catharinae Vadstanensis, Uppsala, 1833
Riant, P., Scandinaves en Terre Sainte, Paris, 1851
Russo, F., Santa Brigida nelle legenda, Lanciano, 1913
Schiller, H., Den heliga Birgitta av Vadstena, Stockholm, 1944
Schönebeck, A., Histoire des Ordres de Chevalerie, Amsterdam, 1692
Stiernman, A., Svecia illustris, Uppsala, 1800
Stolpe, S., Die Offenbarungen der Heiligen Birgitta, Frankfurt, 1961
Surius, L., Commentaries, Rome 1535
Tenzel, W., Monatliche Unterredungen, Berlin, 1697
Theseider, D., I Papi di Avignone, Firenze, 1939
Tigerstedt, E., Svensk Litteraturhistoria, Stockholm, 1960
Toschi, P., La poesia popolare religiosa, Firenze, 1935
Turrecremata, J., Revelationum libri, Roma, 1521
Williamson, B., The Brigittine Order, London, 1922
Würtemberg, M., Konceptgenealogier, Stockholm, 1818